e|Merge

2.0

Developing Youth as Fully Devoted Disciples

Small-Group Leader's Guide for
Older Youth

07 08 09 10 11 12 13 14 15 16—10 9 8 7 6 5 4 3 2 1

Cover Design: Keely Moore

Contents

How to Use This Resource

Congratulations on being called to minister to youth as a small-group leader! As a small-group leader, you will work with students in a personal setting, taking what the youth have learned from the large-group teaching sessions and going deeper through activities, discussion, and Bible study.

This book and accompanying CD-ROM give you lesson plans, handouts, key Scriptures, and discussion questions for thirteen 45-minute sessions with your small group. You'll find at the beginning of each session plan "The Big Idea" (the key teaching for that session), "Session Texts" (the key Scriptures for that session), and "Before You Teach This Lesson," (personal reflection as you prepare for the session).

Each lesson plan then includes the following:

• **Warm-up:** an opening game related to the key teaching for the session.

• **Teaching:** a summary of what youth should learn from that session and why it is important.

• **Handout:** a worksheet that the youth complete individually or in small groups that will get them thinking about the key teaching for that session and how it applies to their lives. Printable PDFs of these handouts are found on the CD-ROM. Information for discussing each question on each handout is provided in this book.

• **Look at the Book:** a short Bible study that explores the key Scriptures for that session.

• **Wrap-up:** a summary of what the youth should take away from the session, and a suggestion for a closing prayer.

The CD-ROM also includes three audio tracks that help you better understand your role as a small-group leader and give you tips on how best to serve the youth in your small group. You can listen to these tracks with a CD or MP3 player.

How to Use the CD-ROM: To listen to the audio tracks, place the CD-ROM in a standard audio CD player. To access the printable handouts or to download MP3 files of the audio tracks, insert the CD-ROM into your computer.

Contagious Faith: Lost

The Big Idea

God loves lost people. Do you? Whenever something is lost, everything stops until it's found. In this session, we'll look at the three stories in **Luke 15** that expose God's heart and God's passion for lost people.

Session Text

• **Luke 15** (The parables of the lost sheep, lost coin, and lost son)

Additional Text

• **Matthew 22:34-40** (The Greatest Commandment)

• **Matthew 28:16-20** (The Great Commission)

Before You Teach This Lesson

Have you ever lost your car keys, cell phone, pet, or wedding ring? If so, you know that when something is lost, everything stops. The urgency of finding what is lost overrides all else.

Here are some questions to ponder as you approach teaching this lesson:

• Do you have friends who are far away from God? If so, what are you doing to actively tell them the message of God?

• Does the thought of sharing your faith excite you or frighten you?

• How passionate would your close friends say you are for lost people?

Warm-up

Discuss the following warm-up questions:

• Who here has had the best week, and why?

• Has there been a time when as a child you found yourself lost? How did that feel? How were you eventually found?

• Have you ever lost an item of great personal value? What emotions did you feel when you discovered it was missing?

The hope is that you'll have some outrageous "lost" stories. Let this warm-up be a time for students to tell their stories and connect with one another on the universal nature of humans to lose things.

Map Quest

<table>
<tr><td>What You'll Need
Copies of "Map Quest" handout (on the CD-ROM)</td></tr>
</table>

Distribute the worksheet. Instruct the youth to locate the spot marked, "You are here" then follow your directions as best they can. Explain that they must listen closely because you will give each direction only once.

Say: "Go three streets north, and turn right. Go two streets, and turn left. Go two lights, then turn south. Stop when you get to the light." These vague instructions should land the students in various spots.

Teaching

God loves lost people even more than we love our lost cell phones, class rings, or keys. God loves lost people so much that God would come to earth to ensure that we would know the way out of our hopelessness and know the way to the heart of God.

When we look at the Great Commandment (**Matthew 22:34-40**) and the Great Commission (**Matthew 28:16-20**), we see that we are to love others and share the love that God has for everyone. We need to sing with the hymn writer John Newton, "I once was lost but now am found," and share our joy with the people around us.

Handout: Contagious Faith

<table>
<tr><td>What You'll Need
Copies of "Contagious Faith" (on the CD-ROM), pens or pencils</td></tr>
</table>

Hand out copies of "Contagious Faith," and give youth time to complete them. Then talk about the worksheet, using these discussion points:

• Describe the person who has made the most impact on your spiritual journey. How did he or she come into your life, and how was God at work in the relationship?

- As a leader, tell how God used the person you identified to make a difference in your life. Invite youth to discuss their experiences.

- Challenge the youth to express their feelings with this person this week, and encourage them in doing so.

- One at a time read the Scripture references, and give the students a chance to articulate the passage in their own words.

Look at the Book

Together, read **Luke 15:1-7** (through the parable of the lost sheep).

Ask:

• Has anyone ever lost a pet? Who has spent the most time looking for their pet? What do you think this story says about God's love for lost people?

Together, read **Luke 15:8-10** (the parable of the lost coin).

Ask:

• Do any of you own a special piece of jewelry or family heirloom? If so, how would you react if you discovered that it was missing? What do you think this story says about God's love for lost people?

Together, read **Luke 15:11-32** (the parable of the lost son).

Ask:

• How, do you think, would your parents react if you told them that you were fed up with their rules and were going to move out of their house? Do you think there is anything that you could ever do that would make your parents (or grandparents, stepparents, or caregivers) stop loving you? What do you think this story says about God's love for lost people?

Wrap-up

Give some time for silent prayer, thanking God for the people who have influenced you on your journey. Ask God for the wisdom and love you need to be that type of an influence other friends.

Contagious Faith: Show

The Big Idea

A saying attributed to St. Francis of Assisi tells us, "Preach the gospel at all times. Use words if necessary." When it comes to sharing our faith, our actions will speak louder than our words. Servant evangelism makes people aware that God loves them, and it tunes their attention in to what you will have to say later.

Session Texts

• **John 15:4-6** (Jesus as the vine, us as the branches)

• **Galatians 5:22-23** (The fruit of the Spirit)

• **1 Thessalonians 1:4-10** (Becoming imitators of the Lord)

Before You Teach This Lesson

When a live plant functions perfectly as designed, it produces fruit. Failure to yield fruit indicates that something is wrong.

Reflect on these questions:

• What are the fruits of your life?

• Have you ever tried to produce fruit without tapping into the vine?

• What is at risk for you as a leader if your relationship remains disconnected for any length of time?

What You'll Need
A list of chosen items for one student, large pictures of those items for the second

---

Warm-up: A Picture Is Worth a Thousand Words

Have two students compete get the other students to guess what they're trying to communicate. The first contestant to get someone to name the item wins.

The first student should describe something by using words, without naming the item.

The second student should wait for a count of ten and then hold up the picture of that item.

For example, the first youth may say, "It flies, has a nest, and lays eggs" to get the group to say the word; then the second youth would hold up a picture of a wasp.

Talk about who had an easier time communicating? Why?

Teaching

The word *show* can imply "an intended production" or "a desired display." We have to realize that once our relationship with God is known, people are tuning in. Our lives become what others will know of a relationship with God.

Handout: Fruit Juice

What You'll Need
Copies of "Fruit Juice" worksheet (on the CD-ROM)

Students sometimes have a difficult time translating the meaning of Scripture from the pages of the Bible into their lives. Give the students some time to work alone, providing some specific situations to ponder (such as winning, losing, friendships, and joking).

Have a volunteer read aloud the Scripture from the top of the handout. Then open some discussion of each of the fruits:

Love: Push them to find applications of love that are more difficult than showing love to their mom or their friends.

Joy: Talk about the difference between joy and happiness. Joy remains solidly positive even through unhappy circumstances.

Peace: This fruit is usually most noticeable when things are not peaceful. When are their lives not peaceful?

Patience: Today's youth get pretty much what they want. How has this cultural phenomenon affected their ability to wait?

Kindness: Specific situations tend to reveal kindness. Talk about the dynamics and difficulties of showing kindness beyond their peers.

Goodness: How hard is it to have a spirit of goodness?

Faithfulness: This fruit often gets attached to marriage. What are some other areas where you can show faithfulness or unfaithfulness?

Gentleness: Gentleness is similar to kindness but less situation specific. do to What would a person have to be considered gentle?

Self-control: Where do you struggle with self-control? What outside factors contribute to that difficulty?

Look at the Book

Have a volunteer read **1 Thessalonians 1:4-10.** Ask:

• In verse 5, does it sound like the gospel was received lightly? How does the gospel that you have responded to have life and power?

Say: "We talked earlier about the reality that when people find out that we claim belief in God, our lives go under the microscope. The same was true for the believers in Thessalonica as well, as we see in verse 7, where Paul says, 'You became an example to all the believers.' Their lives held up to scrutiny because they had received the message with such power that it transformed their lives. "

Ask:

• What danger to you is there when you claim belief in God but don't live it out? *(self-deception, empty living, misdirected life)*

• What danger is there for others when you make those false claims? *(You risk leading others away from following God.)*

Wrap-up

Have the students reflect on these questions:

• If you saw an apple tree that was growing pears, what kind of tree would you say it was? What if it insisted that it was an apple tree despite what kind of fruit you were seeing?

Close in prayer, asking God for the passion to live so that others will look at your lives and see God's love at work.

Contagious Faith: Say

The Big Idea

• "Last night we did this really cool thing at youth group ..."

• "I can't wait for my mission trip this summer ..."

• "I can't go tonight. I'm volunteering at a soup kitchen ..."

• "I know things are tough at home. Can I pray for you?"

Being able to openly declare that they are followers of Jesus is a big step for students. But to help their friends meet Christ, they must be able to verbalize that they live a life transformed by him.

Session Texts

• **Proverbs 15:23** (*Message*): Congenial conversation—what a pleasure! The right word at the right time—beautiful!

• **Acts 3:1-16** (Peter and John heal a beggar with a disability.)

Before You Teach This Lesson

How do your words show people that you are a Christian? How do your conversations reveal that your life has been transformed by Christ?

In this session, you will help youth find ways to share their faith with friends and peers by bringing it up in daily conversation. As you prepare to teach this session, think about ways you express your faith through everyday talk. Think about co-workers and other peers with whom you spend time on a regular basis. What about your conversations with these people would indicate to them that you are a Christian who belongs to a faith community?

Reflect on these questions:

• Whom do you know who does not (or may not) have a relationship with Christ? With which of these people do you have the easiest time talking about your faith? With which of them is talking about your faith most difficult?

• Which aspects of your faith are easiest for you to talk about? Which are most challenging?

Warm-up: Work It In

Beforehand, select a name for each of the following:

<table>
<tr><td>
What You'll Need
Pencil, sheet of paper,
marker, markerboard or large
sheet of paper, Bibles
</td></tr>
</table>

- a fictional character,
- a location,
- an everyday object,
- a food item,
- a vehicle, and
- a verse of Scripture.

Here's an example of a list: Spider-Man, a barbershop, a lawn mower, a casserole, a scooter, and **Micah 6:8.** Write your chosen list on a markerboard or large sheet of paper before the session begins.

Challenge the students to create, either as a group or in pairs, a story that incorporates all of these elements. If all of the youth are working together, have them turn their story into a skit in which each person plays a role. If the students are working in pairs, give them a few minutes to work; then invite each duo to tell its story. Commend the groups on finding creative ways to weave all the items into their stories.

Move on to discussing these questions:

- Which elements did you have the most trouble working into the story?

- What role did the verse of Scripture play in your story? What effect, if any, did the Scripture have on the characters?

Teaching

People talk. The ability to communicate complex ideas to one another through speech and writing is one of the things that set humans apart from other species. And what we say to one another matters. A kind word can make someone's day; a rude insult can ruin it. By mentioning to someone that we are part of a Christian community or talking about some of the ways we've responded to Christ's love, we plant a seed that may some day take root and bear fruit. (See **Matthew 13.**)

In high school, many youth form close relationships with a handful of friends. Teens find safety and support within these friendship "clusters" and are more willing to be honest and make themselves vulnerable among this small group of friends than they would be among a larger peer group. Challenge the students to think about how faith plays a role in their closest friendships (if at all). Which of their close friends have a relationship with Christ or attend church regularly? Which friends might be interested in being a part of the youth group.

Many high-schoolers also spent a great deal of time with groups that have formed around a common interest, such as sports teams or music ensembles. Encourage youth to maintain practices such as prayer and devotional reading when they are on trips with these groups and to be willing to explain what they are doing and why. Often members of groups that work hard toward a common goal have a mutual respect for one another and are willing to learn about one another's passions and interests.

Handout: What I Say

> **What You'll Need**
> Copies of "What I Say"
> worksheet (on the CD-ROM)

Hand out copies of "What I Say," and ask the youth to complete it. Let them work; then talk about their answers, using these discussion points:

1. Ask for volunteers to say which of the items they rated a 4 or 5 and which they rated a 1 or 2. What are the similarities among the items the students were most comfortable talking about? among the items the students were least comfortable talking about?

2. Follow up on this question by asking, "Why?" Are the youth most comfortable talking about their faith when they are among close friends, or among people they don't know very well? Do they need some assurance that the people they're talking to won't ridicule them for talking about church?

3. Again, follow up on this question by asking, "Why?" To whom and in what situations is discussing their faith most difficult? Then ask the youth to talk about situations when they've been able to speak about friends or peers about their beliefs or what was going on at church even though doing so was uncomfortable. How did their friends or peers respond in these situations?

Look at the Book

Ask the youth to read aloud the story of Peter and John healing the beggar who was crippled (**Acts 3:1-10**).

Then say: "Peter and John were just going about their daily routine of praying in the Temple when they saw the beggar who was also crippled sitting at the Temple's gate, asking for donations. The two apostles had no money to give but knew that they could give the beggar something much greater than gold or silver—they healed him on the spot. As they healed the man, Peter proclaimed the name of the one who gave him the power to heal: Jesus Christ."

Ask:

• When do you have opportunities to serve others or perform acts of kindness?

• When you serve others, how can you let people know that you are serving in the name of Christ? *(Assure the students that they don't need to preach a sermon every time they hold a door open for someone. But when they participate in organized service projects through church, they could wear T-shirts identifying the church or simply be prepared to tell anyone who asks why the church has chosen this particular service project, for example.)*

Then ask the youth to read aloud **Acts 3:11-16** (Peter's speech in Solomon's Portico after the healing).

Say: "The people in the Temple, most of whom did not recognize Jesus as the messiah, were astonished by what they saw. Peter boldly told the crowd that they should not be amazed by what he and John had done because he and John hadn't done anything; rather, Christ had worked through them to heal the beggar."

Ask:

• When and how can you give credit to Christ for the good things you are able to do?

• How do your friends and peers know how Christ has changed your life?

Ask a volunteer to read aloud **Proverbs 15:23.** (Use *The Message* if you have it.)

Say: "Every situation is different, and there is no sure-fire way you can plan to talk about your faith with friends and peers. But we need to be mindful of how the Holy Spirit is working in our lives, how Christ has changed our lives, and how the church supports us and helps us grow. With that awareness we can always be ready to tell people why we do what we do, why we believe what we believe, and why we've made a commitment to Christ and our church community. We never know when something we say will be the 'right word at the right time' that will bring someone closer to God."

Wrap-up

Allow the youth to spend a moment in silence, reflecting on how the Holy Spirit is working in their lives, how Christ has changed their lives, and how the church supports them and helps them grow.

Then close in prayer, asking God to give your students the strength, courage, and ability to talk about their relationship with Christ and how it's changed their lives.

The Big Idea

The best way for our friends to be exposed to God is for them to hang out with believers. During this session we will talk about the step of inviting our friends to an event at church, a Christian concert, or another venue where God's message is being shared.

Session Text

- **Mark 1:16-18** (Jesus invites Simon and Andrew to be fishers of people.)

Before You Teach This Lesson

Think about these things:

- What is the most meaningful invitation you've ever received?

- How did you feel when you received that invitation?

- To what event would young people most like to be invited? Why?

- What would make your group a place to which students would enthusiastically invite their friends?

- When is the last time you invited someone to your church? How does the thought of inviting a friend to church make you feel?

- How were you invited into a life of faith?

What You'll Need
Party favors, two pens, two sheets of paper; optional: invitations, pen, stamps

Warm-up: Party Time

Beforehand, send the students invitations to this youth group session via e-mail, telephone, or snail mail.

Divide the youth into two groups. Tell them that they are officially in the party-planning business. Have each group create names and slogans for their businesses. Their project is to create a party that will get the most people to come. Have them think about all the elements that go into planning a party, including what kind of festivity they would have the most fun at and the party they think they could get the most people to. Have them describe the vibe or atmosphere that would be most enjoyable. Give them five minutes to write a description of the party and "sell" it to you as though they were trying to win the bid. Pick a winning team, and hand out party favors.

Teaching

This session attempts to help students feel comfortable and compelled to invite their friends to youth group or to church. Following Jesus means inviting others to join you on the journey. Jesus invited the disciples to follow him. When he invited them, they left what they were doing and followed him. In the same way, he calls us to follow him; and he teaches us how to be "fishers of people." So, following not only means that we choose Jesus; it also means inviting other people to choose the path of following Christ as well.

Inviting people to church doesn't do much good unless we are also committed to hospitality. How do we receive guests into our community? What if you invited someone to come to youth group but you got sick that day and couldn't make it? Say your friend went without you. As a visitor, how would he or she be treated?

Talk about creating a "Don't ditch 'em" policy, by which a visitor is paired up with a "regular." That person acts as a friend to show the newcomer around and make him or her feel welcome.

Handout: Personal Invitation

Hand out copies of the "Personal Invitation" worksheet. Have the students reflect on the printed questions and then write simple, one-sentence statements to

> **What You'll Need**
> Copies of "Personal Invitation" worksheet (on the CD-ROM)

rehearse inviting their unchurched friends to come to church with them.

• How do you feel about inviting a friend to church? *(The youth will probably either say it's no big deal or that they'd be too embarrassed to ask. Affirm both sides of the spectrum. There isn't a right answer.)*

• Why would you invite a friend to go to church with you? *(The students might say something about concerts or the fun they have. They might also describe feeling more secure in the crowd if they*

have a friend with them. Push them to think about the last time they
wanted to invite someone specifically to the love and forgiveness of
Jesus Christ.)

• Suppose you asked a friend to come to church with you and her
response was, "Why should I come?" What would you say to that?
(Help your students articulate why they would want to invite a friend
to church. Is it the community? Is it the music? Is it the love they feel?)

Look at the Book

Have some volunteers tell some of their one-liner invitations from the
handout. Transition to Jesus' instructions to be "fishers of people."
Point out how simply Jesus invited them. He said, "Come, follow
me." Read the Scripture, and talk about the power of an invitation.

To engage the youth with the Scripture passage, have them retell the
story. Start by saying one sentence; then go around the circle having
each student add one more piece of the events described in the story.

After the re-telling discuss these questions:

• What stuck out to you about the Bible story?

• Which character do you most resemble?

• What do you suppose it means to be a "fisher of men and women?"

• How could you be a fisher of people in your school?

• What would our youth group look like if we all took seriously
Jesus' call to invite others to follow him with us?

Wrap-up

To close, go back to the names the youth wrote on index cards in the
"Lost" session, when they named people who need to know the love of
Christ. Ask the youth to spend a minute silently praying for the courage
to invite these friends to church. After the silence, form a circle and
hold hands. Say a prayer that these students would feel comfortable
and compelled to be fishers of people and invite their friends.

Contagious Faith: Tell

The Big Idea

Everyone has a God story. In traditional terms, this story is called a testimony. Some people can tell of dramatic transformations that God has done in their lives; other stories are seemingly simple yet are a powerful witness of God's love. This lesson aims to help students identify their God stories and be able to communicate their experiences in a simple and concise way.

Session Texts

• **Acts 22:6-16** (Paul's experience of Christ on the Damascus road)

• **1 John 1:1-3** (We have heard, seen, and experienced Christ; and now we are telling you so that you too may have that relationship.)

Before You Teach This Lesson

Nearly every day, people tell stories: What did you do today? What happened in the game? What was the movie about? Yet when we're asked about our God story, many of us fall silent, feeling inadequate and not knowing how or where to begin. For some people, the story of Paul's dramatic conversion on the Damascus road is the standard; and who among us has a testimony that comes close to his? But we are not locked into a one-size-fits-all story, especially in relationship to God. God works in our lives in many ways and, yes, in mysterious ways. We are called to pay attention, so that we hear, see, and experience Christ. Then we have not a story but many stories to tell of God!

• Looking back is a good way to see the story. What was your first awareness of God like?

• When did you begin attending church? Why? What kept you coming?

• What hard times have you faced? How did you experience God with you in those difficulties?

• Have you had a time of turning your back on Christ? What happened to turn you around?

• If you could tell only one story about your experience of God in your life, what would you say?

Warm-up: Grab-Bag Story

What You'll Need

Sack of ten small, unrelated items

Tell the teens to pull out an item as the bag is passed to them. The group is to tell one story including each item. The person with the birthday closest to the session's date begins by saying, "Once upon a time . . . " As soon as the first teen has included his or her item, he or she can stop at any point (even in mid-sentence). The next teen must pick up the storyline and weave in his or her item. The rest of the youth do likewise. If a teen gets stuck, wait a few seconds before moving on; then come back to him or her. If the pressure appears to be too much for someone, ask for a volunteer to finish the story with that item.

Teaching

As Christians, we have good news! We can't keep it to ourselves. Since we have experienced God's love, we need to tell others, especially our friends, so that they too can know God.

What You'll Need

Copies of "What's Your Story?" (on the CD-ROM), pens or pencils

Handout: What's Your Story?

Distribute the handouts. Have the youth complete it on their own then, for the last part, with a partner. Discuss their answers.

Look at the Book

Here's another chance for the youth to practice storytelling. Ask the students to tell you what they know about Saul (later Paul). Encourage them in the telling of the story even if they get details and order wrong. Remind the youth of Saul's role in the persecutions of Christians; tell them to read **Acts 9:1-19** aloud section by section. Then go through the story verbally to fill in details and correct the order if need be.

Wrap-up

Say: "All of us have God stories. Some people haven't realized they have them; but those of us who've recognized God's love feel a need to tell others. We can't keep it to ourselves—and we shouldn't! This week, find a way to tell someone. Who needs to hear a God story from you?"

The Big Idea

Perhaps the most mystifying part of sharing our faith is all of the varied teachings on sealing some kind of deal. You might have heard of the Four Spiritual Laws, The Roman Road, or The Sinner's Prayer as tools for conversion. All of these methods focus on a moment of commitment or a decision to choose to follow Jesus. While Jesus does call us to choose his way, there is no magic formula for saying yes. We want to create relationship with people where they come to know who Jesus is because of the lives we live. We want to connect with people so that they feel safe enough to ask us questions about faith. We want to reach a point with people where we can ask them to choose to follow Christ.

Session Texts

• **Luke 15:17-21** (The prodigal son returns home.)

• **John 3:16** ("For God so loved the world.")

• **Romans 3:23** (All have sinned.)

• **1 John 1:9** (If we confess, God will forgive us.)

Before You Teach This Lesson

This session is hard, because we want to know for sure that the young people we mentor have "sealed the deal" with Jesus. The easy thing to do is give someone a formula for getting saved; then we know we've "got them." But the truth is that as hard as we work to do so, we don't convert anyone—the Holy Spirit brings about conversion in the hearts of people. Our job is "show and tell" about Jesus and his love for us.

Think about the moment or period of time when you remember making a decision to follow Jesus. Did you say a special prayer, or did you simply recognize your state of sin and need of Jesus? It's important to wrap your head around the idea that we are not the converters and that the Holy Spirit is the one to change our hearts. In this way, you can help youth feel free from the burden of getting people to confess and empower them to live a contagious faith that leads the way to Jesus.

Warm-up: D.T.R. (Define the Relationship)

This game is a funny way to help youth look at the ways that they attempt to define their relationships. Ask for six volunteers, and instruct them to divide into pairs. You'll need two guy-girl pairs and one same-gender pair.

Assign each pair one of the following labels: "BFF" (best friends forever), "Going Out," "Just Friends." Have the pairs roleplay a conversation to define the relationship according to their assignment. Encourage them to look back on their younger days and their attempts to define their growing relationships. They can imagine that they are in elementary school or junior high—or even in high school.

Here is an example of a BFF roleplay:

> **Carrie:** Hey, Sam, I wrote you a note. Here it is.
> **Sam:** Thanks. Should I read it?
> **Carrie:** Go ahead, I guess.
> **Sam:** "Sam, will you be my best friend? Yes, no, or maybe." That's so sweet, Carrie. Of course you're my best friend. Let's go buy a BFF necklace!

Teaching

Over the last few weeks, you've learned that God loves lost people. You've learned how to show lost people that you're a Christian. You've learned how to say that you love Jesus. You've rehearsed some ways to invite your non-believing friends to come to church with you. You've practiced telling your God story. So how can you be sure that they are going to become Christian after you've put all of this effort into that goal? How do you know that they have found a friend in Christ?

At certain points in any relationship, you have to name it. You are best friends, acquaintances, strangers, partners, a couple, teammates, family, or some other descriptor of a relationship. How do you get friends you bring to church to define their relationship with Jesus?

What You'll Need

Copies of the "The Lost Son Came Home" (on the CD-ROM), pens or pencils

Handout: The Lost Son Came Home

Distribute copies of the handout; ask the youth to individually read the Scripture and write their answers to the questions.

Love is a decision. Too often, the word *love* is tossed around lightly to connote misty-eyed emotion that you either feel or don't feel. But love is the greatest choice a person can make. When it comes to our relationship with Christ, we have to decide that we will give our lives to loving him and loving others.

One way to give people the language of choosing Jesus is to help them give all of what they know of themselves to all they know of God.

Look at the Book

Read aloud **John 3:16.** Ask:

• How can you communicate this love that God has for the world?

• Imagine a conversation with a non-believing friend. What do you say? How does he or she respond?

Read aloud **Romans 3:23.** Ask:

• Why does knowing we are all in the same sinner boat feel good?

• How can you tell that good news to a friend? What would you say?

Read aloud **1 John 1:9**. Say: "Put this promise in your own words, and memorize it. Let it be sealed on your heart so that you can share it with your friends."

Wrap-up

Say: "The tools that we've received over these last few weeks will only bring people closer to God if we use them. Remember that God loves lost people and so should you. Practice your faith so that all may see your life and want what you've got! Get comfortable talking about the things you do with the church or the ways God works in your life so that you can speak freely and naturally about them. Invite your non-churched friends to youth group. And support them in the process of giving all they know of themselves to all they know of God!"

Pray for the courage and vulnerability to help people come to know God. Ask the Lord to show you the faces of people to share your faith with and give you the strength, actions, and words to make a difference.

Scars: Stop the Bleeding

The Big Idea

Students have to realize that everyone has scars, whether emotional or physical. Acknowledging that they are hurting is the first step toward bringing a time of hurting to an end. They are not alone, and they can find solace in the realization of God's presence.

Session Texts

• **Psalm 31:9-11** (Be gracious to me, O LORD, for I am in distress.)

• **Psalm 139:1-5** (O LORD, you have searched me and known me.)

Before You Teach This Lesson

Be prepared to deal with startling honesty from your students during this lesson. Determine in advance to what degree you are willing to disclose about your own pain. Prayerfully consider these questions:

• What pain have you experienced in your life?

• What kind of pain have you handled well?

• Have you ever handled your pain poorly?

• Does any pain in your life remain unresolved?

Warm-up: Operation

> **What You'll Need**
> The Milton Bradley board game called Operation

Bring in or borrow the game Operation. Allow everyone to take turns on the various surgeries. While you play, discuss the following questions:

• Has anyone here ever had an operation? (If not, move to surgeries in the immediate family.)

• How did you feel before the operation? Were you nervous?

• Did you at any point consider not getting the surgery and instead dealing with the pain of an unresolved medical issue?

Teaching

We all have experienced pain, if not in the present then certainly in the past. Often we hide our pain, either from embarrassment or from fear of rejection should anyone discover the problem.

Open and honest communication with our peers reminds us that everyone experiences pain. We are not alone in experiencing pain, and as Christians we not alone in getting through our pain. God, who knows us deeply and intimately, is with us, supporting us always.

Handout: Heart on Your Sleeve

What You'll Need
Copies of "Heart on Your Sleeve" handout (on the CD-ROM), pens or pencils

Say: "Write in the heart the things that matter to you—including things that cause you pain. Start at the edges with the things that you make readily accessible to others, like your taste in movies and music. As you get closer to the center, write things that are more personal but more important, such as how you view yourself, heartaches, and the stuff that hurts."

Debrief with these questions:

• How easy was writing around the edges of your heart?

• How easy was writing as you got closer to the middle?

• How many of you thought of something that you weren't willing to write down?

Look at the Book

Have a volunteer read **Psalm 31:9-11.**

Ask:

• Do any of you write in a journal?

Discuss some of the positive aspects of writing in a journal. Many of the psalms are essentially David's journal entries, where his heart is able to cry louder than his voice. We find in many psalms emotions laid bare in this fashion.

Ask:

• What is healthy about this outlet of expressing pain?

• What would be unhealthy about this method if it were the only outlet?

• Have any of you experienced pain at the level described here by David?

• How did you process it?

Encourage the youth to always seek help with their pain, no matter how capable they may feel about handling it themselves. Even if they are capable, their willingness to be open and honest about their pain may help someone who has a similar struggle.

Wrap-up

Have a student read **Psalm 139:1-5.**

Ask:

• What is comforting about having someone know you so completely? *(no fear about being honest in the relationship; security)*

• God knows us this intimately yet still loves us and desires to be in relationship with us. How does knowledge this make you feel?

Scars: Find the Healing

The Big Idea

The acknowledgment of pain serves only as the foundation for healing. Without intentionally constructive progress over time, wounds will remain open and become even more painful than the original injury.

Session Texts

• **Proverbs 3:5-8** (Turn to God, not just your own insight, to find healing.)

• **John 5:5-9** (Jesus heals a man who could not walk.)

Before You Teach This Lesson

Realize the tenderness of an unattended wound in the life of a youth. Be delicate with this instruction. As you prepare for this session, consider these questions:

• When you have struggled to deal with pain in the past, what was your turning point?

• What were some things that might have delayed you from seeking healing?

• Is becoming comfortable with a wound possible?

Warm-up: I Didn't See It 'Til It Hit Me!

Play a quick round of "I've Got a Cooler Scar Than That." Have a student show physical scars and tell the stories behind them. Examples include dog bites, tree saws, shark bites, and "didn't see it 'til it hit me" stories.

Debrief with these questions:

• How long did it take for you to treat your wound?

• What would have happened if you had let the wound go untreated?

Teaching

An untreated physical wound can quickly get ugly. Infection can set in, and soon more of the body is affected by what was likely an initially containable ailment. Emotional injuries carry the same dangers. Without attention, they can begin to affect other areas of your life. Friends, family, even your relationship with God can suffer if an emotional wound gets pushed aside.

What You'll Need
Copies of "Self-Medicating" worksheet (on the CD-ROM), pens or pencils

---

Handout: Self-Medicating

The point of this exercise is to show that we are not prepared to handle every situation. Sometimes, though, how we respond in a difficult situation can set the table for recovery.

Ask these questions:

• These situations may never happen to you, but how did you feel when you thought about facing an unexpected situation?

• Did you feel equipped or qualified to deal with any of these scenarios?

• What were common, critical things to do in each situation? *(seeking qualified help, remaining with your friend, offering support)*

Look at the Book

Have a volunteer read **John 5:5-9.** Ask:

• Why on earth would Jesus ask a man who had been ill for thirty-eight years whether he wanted to be made well?

• The man did not directly answer Jesus' question. Do you find that way of responding odd?

• How have thirty-eight years of dealing with illness affected his approach to getting well?

Say: "This man has a clear need, but it has become unclear to him. He has lost sight of a life of health, instead fixating on the difficulties of his illness. His existence has become intertwined with the thing that separates him from normalcy, to the point that, when Jesus asks whether he would like to become well, he replies with an explanation of his predicament."

Ask:

• How has this man's inability to deal with his illness taken his life hostage?

Discuss with the students the danger of not processing an illness (physical or spiritual). Oftentimes, not dealing with something can make the problem the focus of our lives (as in this man's case). But if we seek God's healing, we can deal with the pain and move on with God's help.

Wrap-up

Have a volunteer read **Proverbs 3:5-8.**

Explain that God's healing is not like magic. The process can be difficult and take time. But we are not alone, and God's love is steadfast. The healing will come; we can trust God.

Close with this exercise of solidarity for your group. Remind them that oftentimes, they can be the first step of healing for others in their group. Encourage the students to respond to your questions in the following litany by saying, "We will trust in the Lord":

• In whom will you trust? *(We will trust in the Lord.)*

• On whom will you rely? *(We will trust in the Lord.)*

• Whom will you acknowledge? *(We will trust in the Lord.)*

• Who will make straight your paths? *(We will trust in the Lord.)*

• Whom will you fear? *(We will trust in the Lord.)*

• Who will heal you? *(We will trust in the Lord.)* Amen.

Bling: Give With Faith

The Big Idea

A giving spirit is a critical attribute of persons wishing to deepen their Christian walk. Learning key scriptural concepts will help youth cultivate the intentionality and attitudes toward giving shown in the Old and New Testaments.

Session Texts

- **Genesis 14:19-20** (Melchizedek blesses Abram, who gives him a tenth of everything.)

- **Genesis 28:20-22** (Jacob vows to give God a tenth of all that God has blessed him with.)

- **1 Corinthians 16:1-3** (Paul instructs the Corinthians to give money to their church.)

- **2 Corinthians 9:7-8** (God loves a cheerful giver.)

Before You Teach This Lesson

Youth grow up in extremely diverse circumstances regarding the subject of tithing and giving money to the church. Some families are fully ten-percent givers or more. Some split their tithes between local churches and missions or social organizations. Some give little or not at all.

Thinking over your experience with tithing, consider these questions:

- In your upbringing, what did your family feel was its responsibility to God financially?

- What are your personal beliefs about tithing and the responsibility of the church as it handles our tithes?

- How familiar are you with the Scriptures that deal with tithing?

- Did these Scriptures shape your original beliefs about tithing, or have your beliefs formed out of what you already "knew" about it?

Warm-up: Bean Counters

Jar full of jellybeans

Present a big jar of jellybeans. You should know in advance how many jellybeans are in the jar. Have the students come up one at a time and remove what they feel is ten percent of the jellybeans. They should count what they take out and then put them back in the jar. After everyone has had chance to go, tell them how many jellybeans were in the jar.

Ask:

• Who came closest to ten percent? Who was the farthest?

• Was it difficult to figure out how much ten percent was? Was it more than what you expected, or less?

Teaching

Tithing is truly about joyful giving. We must get past the legalistic argument to tithe and realize that the joy of giving reflects a healthy relationship with God. As we grow in our relationship with God, we give our tithe before we buy anything else. This prioritization is the surest sign of faith; no faith is involved in giving out of what's left.

Handout: Earned and Burned

What You'll Need
Copies of "Earned and Burned" handout (on the CD-ROM), pens or pencils

Hand out copies of "Earned and Burned," and let the youth complete it. Then discuss their answers to the three questions:

1. Get them talking about how they spend their money. Don't focus yet on any responsibility. Look for their leisure spending.

2. Point out how a job and a car often create financial responsibility. Suddenly gas, insurance, and sometimes even a partial car payment eat into what a student used to be able to spend at will.

3. Reintroduce the idea of giving ten percent. Compare it to the percentage they spent on themselves in the first question. Discuss family tithing practices. Do their parents give to the church? How much? How often? Do their parents attempt to instill tithing practices in them?

Bling: Give With Faith

31

Look at the Book

Have two volunteers read **Genesis 14:19-20** and **Genesis 28:20-22.**

Ask:

• Who are the characters in each of these Scriptures?

• What do Abram and Jacob both do in these verses? *(give back to God)*

• Do they seem obligated to do so?

Say: "We see here the essence of giving out of faith. The Law hasn't even been written yet, but these men find joy in returning to God out of what they have been given. Their giving, along with the agricultural tithe we find later in Levitical law (**Leviticus 27:30-33**), gives us our model of giving ten percent back to God."

Have two volunteers read **1 Corinthians 16:1-3** and **2 Corinthians 9:7.**

Ask:

• How do these verses echo the spirit of giving found in the Old Testament Scriptures we read a few minutes ago?

• What did Paul mean by "according to his income" in First Corinthians? Do you think he was referencing the ten-percent principle, or leaving the door open wide for even more giving?

Say, "Our faith is not dependent on our giving, but our giving is a reflection of the depth of our faith."

Wrap-up

Direct the students in silent prayer. Tell the youth: "Thank God for all that you have been given. Now ask God to show you one area where you have been holding back from giving. Ask for the ability to open up and give freely. Ask for joy."

Close in a group prayer, asking for continued guidance and the faith to find joy in giving not just financially but in all areas of life.

Bling: Invest With Hope

The Big Idea

Debt steals from tomorrow. In contrast, God offers us a future of hope. When we invest our lives and our resources in God's kingdom, we are preparing for the future instead of stealing from it.

Session Text

- **Matthew 25:14-30** (The Master rewards the two who have invested wisely; the third, who hid his talent, is punished.)

Before You Teach This Lesson

Jesus' parable of the talents is easy to read as an advertisement for an investment company. Instead, Jesus is talking about investing in the present and coming kingdom of heaven (**Matthew 24–25**). Prior to this passage, he speaks of the Second Coming and the necessity of being ready (the wise and foolish bridesmaids, the judgment and the separation of the sheep from the goats). So we can view the parable of the talents as a continuation of Jesus' teachings on investing our lives, including our resources, in the Kingdom, both present and coming.

You, as a small-group leader, are choosing to invest your life in these youth, helping to bring them to Kingdom-living. Your time, your love, your prayer, and probably at times your money are your investment. Because you have been faithful, God will bring about the return. Consider these questions:

- Who has invested in you? How have those investments paid off in your faith and your life?

- God has entrusted you with talents and resources. Name several ways you are blessed.

- How are you investing those gifts?

- What talent or resource are you hoarding or hiding?

- Are you investing your talents and resources in anything that is opposed to God's kingdom?

- If you could give the youth investment advice, what would you say?

Warm-up: That's Good, That's Bad

The goal is to help older youth begin to think about decisions and consequences, especially as they relate to the use of money or time.

Have one youth be a commentator who says, "That's good" or "That's bad" alternately to whatever someone else says. Ask the other youth to spin out a conversation, alternating between the good consequences and the bad in a counter response. Keep the same commentator, but more than one youth can contribute. Here's an example:

> **Youth:** I finally got those tickets to the concert.
> **Commentator:** That's good.
> **Youth:** No, that's bad because I already spent the money I had saved for the tickets, and now I'll have to borrow.
> **Commentator:** Oh, that's bad.
> **Youth:** No, that's good because now I'll be motivated to look for a part-time job.
> **Commentator:** Yes, that's good.
> **Youth:** No, that's bad because I'll have to work on weekends.
> **Commentator:** That is bad.
> **Youth:** No, that's good because . . .

Teaching

We are constantly making decisions on how to spend our money and time. Some of us give away our power to decide and just go with what the media tell us is cool, what our friends have, or how we feel at the moment. Deciding faithfully is not always easy—one reason God helps us through the Bible, church teachings, the support of other Christians, and our abilities to reason and learn from the experiences of others as well as our own. If we slide into debt, however, we will find ourselves weighed down by growing obligations and unable to choose positive and God-directed ways to live both now and in the future. A life buried in debt doesn't easily see the light of hope.

What You'll Need

Copies of "What Does It Mean?" (on the CD-ROM), pencils, at least one calculator that has exponents *or* a computer with Web access

---

Handout: What Does It Mean?

Hand out copies of the worksheet, and let the youth complete it. If you cannot obtain a calculator that can multiply using exponents, use savings calculators and credit-card interest calculators on the Web.

You might invite a financial planner or banker to talk with the teens.

Look at the Book

Direct the youth to read silently **Matthew 25:14-30.** Then ask for four volunteers to act out the parable as one person reads it aloud, allowing time between for the actors to perform. Encourage the dramatists to be creative, while also sticking to the basic story.

After the reading, ask:

• What things might the word *talent* in the parable stand for? *(money, time, talents in the modern sense, our lives, opportunities, blessings)*

• The master made an investment in three servants; two of them also made investments. What does investing mean? *(putting your resources to work in ways that have potential for a positive increase)*

• What does "return on investment" (ROI) mean? *(what you get back from the investment; what returns to you because of your action)*

• Why, do you think, was the master so hard on the third servant? He got his initial investment back OK.

• Seeing this parable as a story of God and us, what are your thoughts?

Wrap-up

When you look at your life, God has given you so much: You have time, money, talents, opportunities, and blessings. But if you try to keep these to yourself, if you try to bury them, rather than share them, you've missed the point. These gifts from God are for you to invest to help bring about God's wonderful kingdom for all. Look for the places God challenges you to invest to help people, to care for creation, to make a difference. Don't fall into the trap of thinking you need more; don't fall for easy money and other kinds of indebtedness. Debt steals from the future; debt robs you of your ability to live with hope. In contrast, however, when you invest the gifts God has given you, you help create a future of hope for others as well as for yourself.

Bling: Live With Love

The Big Idea

God asks us to use money wisely and faithfully. As Christians, we need to let love to be the guiding factor in all of our financial decisions.

Session Texts

• **Isaiah 55:2** (God's wisdom on spending)

• **Luke 3:7-8a; 10-14** (John the Baptist's instructions on managing our resources in a just way)

• **Luke 10:30-35** (the parable of the Good Samaritan)

Before You Teach This Lesson

Age-old sayings tell us that money makes the world go round and that possession is nine-tenths of the law. Ads tell us that we must acquire certain possessions. But the livelihood and wellness of many people depends on how we use our money.

No matter how much we're told that the money in our bank accounts is ours to use as we please, Christians must affirm that money—like all resources—ultimately belongs to God. God entrusts us with money and property with the expectation that we will use it wisely and faithfully.

How faithfully do you use the resources that have been entrusted to you? Reflect on these questions as you prepare to teach this session:

• How do you decide whether to spend your money on something? Whom do you consult? What factors do you weigh? How does your faith play a role in your decisions? Does your decision making depend on the cost of an item that you're considering buying?

• What were the wisest purchases that you ever made? the most foolish?

• What barriers—such as debt and foolish purchases—have prevented you from using your money faithfully in service of God and others?

• How do you discipline yourself to use money wisely and faithfully?

Warm-up: Smart Money

What You'll Need
Copies of the "Smart Money" handout (on the CD-ROM), pens or pencils

Hand out copies of "Smart Money," and let the youth complete it individually. Then go over their answers:

1. Ask the youth why they chose to spend their money on certain items or causes. What factors influenced their decisions? Aside from the possibilities listed, in what ways did they decide to use their money?

2. Talk about what makes a particular purchase wise or foolish. Use examples of wise and foolish purchases that you've made. Ask the students what they can learn from purchases that they made in the past that will help them spend more wisely in the future.

3. List the factors on a large writing surface. Challenge the youth to think of the three most important factors in a spending decision.

Teaching

In the previous sessions, we looked at tithing as an act of faith and at investing as an act of hope. This session looks at the third, and greatest, of Paul's ultimate values from **1 Corinthians 13:13,** which is love. Our love—for God, for others, and for ourselves—should guide all of our decisions, including our financial decisions.

Our love for God should make us want to give generously to our church, but it should also give us the courage to forgo some of our wants and give graciously to others. Such love may involve helping out a friend or family member who's in a bind, lending a few bucks to a stranger who's lost his or her wallet, or donating to a worthy cause. We need to make wise choices with our money so that we are prepared to give when an opportunity arises. If we buy things we don't need, we won't be able to donate to a relief agency in the wake of a natural disaster, buy a soft drink or cup of coffee for a friend who's had a bad day, or respond when the church is raising funds for a new ministry.

Handout: Budget

What You'll Need
Copies of the "Budget" handout (on the CD-ROM), pens or pencils, play money

Divide the youth into two groups, or "families," and give each family a copy of the Budget handout. Assign each family a different monthly income that falls between $2000 and $5000, after taxes. Challenge the families to use the amounts listed on the handout to determine how they will use their income. Tell them that they must pay for at least food and a place to live. Also suggest that they tithe ten percent and invest ten percent. Beyond those parameters, the families may use their money as they please. Families can determine which members are adults and children.

Give the families ten minutes to work. As they do so, go to each family and tell them things that have "come up." You might say, "The church is asking members to pledge money to launch a ministry to college students" or "Your cousin lost his job and can't pay for food and rent. He wants to move in with you; if you take him in, you'll have to pay for his food." The youth can choose whether to respond to these challenges.

After ten minutes, invite each family to talk about their budget, the decisions made, and how they responded to the situations that came up. Ask the youth how love influenced their decisions. Then ask:

• What was most challenging about making your budget? What were you unable to pay for that you would've liked to have?

• What did you learn from this activity about managing your money and using your money faithfully?

• Read **Isaiah 55:2.** In what ways did your family spend money on things that don't satisfy? How did your family invest in "rich food"? *(Explain that the "rich food" the prophet speaks of is life with God.)*

• Read **Luke 10:30-35.** What can we learn from the Samaritan in this story about letting love influence how we use our money?

• Imagine that you lost everything you owned and had $1000 to start buying back your possessions. What would you buy back? Why?

Look at the Book

Ask volunteers to read aloud **Luke 3:7-8a, 10-14.** Say, "John the Baptist was eccentric, to say the least—he chose a life of poverty." Tell the students that Matthew and Mark both describe John as clothed in "camel's hair with a leather belt around his waist," and say that he "at locusts and wild honey." Assure the youth that God does not ask everyone to live in the desert, wearing uncomfortable clothes, and eating honey-coated grasshoppers for every meal. Nonetheless, John the Baptist's teaching is consistent with what Jesus would later proclaim and is important for Christians still today.

Ask a volunteer to re-read verse 11. Say: "Here, John teaches the crowd not to hoard possessions and not to be wasteful. If we cling to things that we don't need, we miss opportunities to lovingly give of what we have to others." (As time permits, also read **Exodus 16:13-21,** the story of the manna from heaven. Point out how God allowed the people to consume only what they needed, no more and no less.) Challenge the youth to think of something that they own but do not need or something that they have too much of. How could these things be put to better use?

Then ask a volunteer to re-read **Luke 3:13-14.** Ask:

• What do you think being "satisfied with your wages" means?

• Suggest to the youth that being satisfied with our wages does not mean that we shouldn't work hard and invest wisely to earn money. Rather, as John suggests, we should not acquire wealth dishonestly or by taking advantage of others. Also note that Jewish law prohibits charging interest on loans (at least loans made to other Jews). As time permits, have the youth read **Deuteronomy 23:19-20.**

Say: "Love, not personal gain, should guide how we make financial decisions. We need to be honest with ourselves about what we do and do not need, and we need to be mindful of the needs of others."

Wrap-up

Say: "Composing a budget or following a set of rules for spending and investing can help us make better decisions. But more important to our financial planning is an attitude that God is in control and will provide."

Read aloud **Matthew 6:25-33.** Say: "Jesus assures us that the Father loves us and will provide for us. With that assurance, we need to listen to God when we decide how to use our money, trusting that the Lord will give us what we need."

Close in prayer, asking God for the courage and wisdom to make godly financial decisions.

Elevate: Going Down?

The Big Idea

Friends have an extraordinary influence on our values and decisions. For many people, friends have a greater influence on them than their parents, teachers, and even God. Because they can have such an impact on our lives, peers are in a unique position to lift us up or bring us down. We need to be careful not to allow friends to bring us down.

Session Texts

• **Proverbs 12:26:** The righteous gives good advice to friends, but the way of the wicked leads astray.

• **Proverbs 13:20:** Whoever walks with the wise becomes wise, but the companion of fools suffers harm.

• **Proverbs 22:24-25:** Make no friends with those given to anger, and do not associate with hotheads, or you may learn their ways and entangle yourself in a snare.

• **Matthew 9:9-13** (Jesus calls the tax collector Matthew to follow him.)

• **Matthew 11:19:** "The Son of Man came eating and drinking, and they say, 'Look, a glutton and a drunkard, a friend of tax-collectors and sinners!' Yet wisdom is vindicated by her deeds."

• **Matthew 18:15-17** (on reproving someone who has sinned against us)

• **Luke 17:2:** "It would be better for you if a millstone were hung around your neck and you were thrown into the sea than for you to cause one of these little ones to stumble."

Before You Teach This Lesson

Think about which people have had the greatest impact, positive or negative, on your life. Then reflect on the following questions as you prepare to teach this session:

• Who were your best friends when you were in high school?

• Which of these friends had a positive effect on your attitudes, behavior, and maturity? Which had a negative effect?

• When has a friend pressured or tempted you to act irresponsibly or put you in a troublesome situation? How did you react?

• When you were in high school, how did you handle negative pressure from friends? When did you give in? When did you resist? Who or what gave you the strength and courage to resist?

Warm-up: Good Friend, Bad Friend

Begin your time together by discussing the following questions:

> **What You'll Need**
> Marker, large writing surface

• When has a close friend tempted you to do something you knew was wrong? How did you respond?

• When have you done something that you knew was wrong so that you could impress a friend or improve your social status?

Ask the students to brainstorm a list of negative behaviors that a friend might pressure them to engage in. (Examples include smoking pot, skipping class, and going to a party without a parent's permission.) Write these behaviors on a markerboard or large sheet of paper.

Then have the students pair off. (If you have an odd number of youth, you'll need to be someone's partner.) Have each pair select one of the subjects on your list and prepare a brief skit in which one person pressures the other to do something that he or she knows is wrong. Give the pairs a few minutes to prepare; then have each pair act out its scenario for the others. After each performance, ask:

• How realistic, do you think, was this scenario? [Keeping in mind your group's comfort level, allow volunteers to talk about times when they've been in a similar situation.]

• What did [name of person trying to resist the pressure] do to resist his or her friend's pressure?

• What would you have done if you were in the same situation as [name of person trying to resist the pressure]?

Teaching

Supportive, affirming friendships are crucial for teen development. But not all friendships are that way; some can become destructive. Among teen friends, behavior is contagious. Researchers have found:

• Behavioral problems among seventh graders increase when they have stable friendships with ill-mannered peers.

• Early adolescents are most likely to become substance abusers if their best friends are substance abusers.

• Adolescents who felt rejected in primary school often join delinquent groups in middle school or junior high for a sense of belonging.

Youth need to be aware that their friends have a significant influence on their lives and behavior, and they should not take their friends' influence for granted. Many high school youth form friendships based on shared interests and activities, such as sports, music, and drama, as well as youth group. But common interests do not always mean common values. Inevitably, many teens will find themselves in situations where their friends pressure them to do things that are contrary to the beliefs and moral standards they claim as Christians. Older youth need to remember their identities as followers of Christ in all situations so that they can set limits and know when to walk away from a bad situation.

What You'll Need
Copies of "Know When to Walk Away" handout (on the CD-ROM), pens or pencils

---

Handout: Know When to Walk Away

Hand out copies of the "Know When to Walk Away," and let the youth complete it. Then talk about each question:

1. Which behaviors are most common? Which are hardest to walk away from? To make the discussion more interesting, you might name some of the pressures that were common when you were in high school. Ask the youth whether this pressure most frequently comes from friends or from other peers. Ask them to think of friends who help them deal with or resist pressure.

2. Allow volunteers to say how they rated each item. Which factors have the greatest influence on their decisions? Which factors *should* have the greatest influence on their decisions?

3. Ask the students to come to a consensus on the best way to handle a friend who continually pressures them to behave irresponsibly. If they decide that it would be best to distance themselves from their friend, move on to question 4 as a follow-up.

4. Encourage creativity. Answers can include praying for that person or being available if he or she needs help.

Look at the Book

Say, "Jesus was well known and often criticized for having questionable friendships." Read aloud **Matthew 11:19.** To show how Jesus defended his relationships with these seemingly seedy friends, have a youth read aloud the call of Matthew the tax collector (**Matthew 9:9-13**).

Say: "During his earthly ministry, Jesus was all about healing. Through his teaching, his miracles, and his interactions with others, he offered grace and forgiveness to sinners who needed to be reconciled with their families, their communities, and God. He also set an example for successive generations of Christians to follow. So shouldn't we be hanging out with the shadiest, most morally depraved people we can find?

"Yes, and no. While Jesus was a positive influence on these friends, he didn't allow these friends to be a negative influence on him. We should always strive to set a good example for our friends and to lead them toward positive and fulfilling behavior, but we also need to recognize when our friends are having a negative impact on us. This danger may be peer pressure and temptation or ending up in situations where trouble is likely to ensue. The Bible warns us against hanging out with people who would have a negative influence on our behavior."

Ask a volunteer to read aloud **Proverbs 13:20; 22:24-25.**

Then say: "We have to use discernment on when to establish distance between ourselves and friends who are having a negative influence on us. Jesus gives us some guidelines for doing so."

Ask a volunteer to read aloud **Matthew 18:15-17** (Jesus' teaching on reproving someone who has sinned against us).

Say: "This Scripture isn't exactly about friends who are having a negative influence on us, but it is about knowing when to draw the line. If a friend continues to pressure you to act irresponsibly or put you in troublesome situations and if you are unable to have positive effect on this friend's behavior, you need to walk away. You can and should continue to pray for this person, and you should be available if this friend comes to you for help; but you have to set limits.

"And we, in turn, must work hard to have a positive influence on our friends and peers."

Ask a volunteer to read aloud **Proverbs 12:26** and another to read aloud **Luke 17:2.**

Then say: "We must always be mindful of what effect our actions and behaviors have on others. We need to make sure that we set a good example, that we don't encourage others to act irresponsibly, and that we do our best to follow the teachings of Christ."

Wrap-up

Summarize this session by reviewing these points:

• Our friends have a big influence on our decisions.

• We need to distance ourselves from friends who continually pressure us to act irresponsibly.

• We can continue to love and care for a friend, even if we have to walk away from that person.

• We must do our best to have a positive influence on our friends.

Close in prayer, thanking God for the gift of friends and asking God for wisdom and discernment when it comes to our relationships with friends, particularly those friends who might have a negative effect on our behavior.

Elevate: Going Up?

The Big Idea

Friends have an extraordinary influence on our values and decisions. For many people, friends have a greater influence on them than their parents, teachers, and even God. Because they can have such an impact on our lives, peers are in a unique position to lift us up or bring us down. We need to be careful not to allow friends to bring us down.

Session Text

• **Ruth 1:1-18** (Ruth and Naomi)

• **1 Samuel 18:1-9; 20:12-42** (David and Jonathan)

• **Proverbs 17:17:** A friend loves at all times.

• **John 15:13** (No greater love than to lay down one's life for friends)

Before You Teach This Lesson

Think about which friends have had the most positive effect on your life. Then reflect on these questions:

• Who were your best friends when you were in high school?

• Which of these friends had a positive effect on your attitudes, behavior, and maturity? How did they have a positive effect?

• How do your friends today support you and sustain you?

• In what ways do you support and sustain your friends?

Warm-up: Create a Best Friend

> **What You'll Need**
> Markers, at least one large sheet of paper; optional: markerboard

Ask the students to spend a few minutes in silence, reflecting on these questions:

• Who are your closest friends? What makes these friends special?

• How have your close friends helped you mature as a person and in your relationship to God?

• How do you help your friends grow in faith?

If you have eight or more youth, divide them into two groups; make them same-sex groups if you can.

Give the youth a large sheet of paper, and set out plenty of colored markers. (If you have multiple groups, give each group a large sheet of paper.) Instruct the students to work together to draw the "perfect friend" on the paper. If the sheet is large enough, you might have the youth begin by tracing one member of the group.

The challenge will be for youth to illustrate traits such as loyalty or sacrifice. They may do so by drawing something on the friend's hand, putting the friend in certain situations, or emphasizing certain parts of the body, such as the heart or brain or hands. Allow them to be creative, and offer suggestions only if they're stuck.

Give the students plenty of time to work; then ask them to name the qualities most everyone agreed on. List these qualities on a markerboard or large sheet of paper.

Teaching

The value of a true best friend cannot be understated. A strong friendship will raise one's self-esteem, improve one's social skills, and enable one to better handle stress. Of course, youth must be able to identify true friendships. Close friends must be able to trust each other and be willing to make sacrifices for each other. A good friend must also live up to **Proverbs 17:17a:** "A friend loves at all times."

Scripture is rich with stories that illustrate the value of a good friend, most notably the stories of Ruth and Naomi and of David and Jonathan. Though your students live in a much different world than that of these biblical heroes, they can nonetheless learn from the loyalty, trust, and selflessness demonstrated by Ruth, Naomi, David, and Jonathan. Youth should both look for such qualities in a friend and strive to model these qualities themselves.

Handout: Going Up?

What You'll Need
Copies of "Going Up?"
worksheet (on the CD-ROM),
pens or pencils

Hand out copies of the sheet, and let the youth work on it. Discuss each question:

1. Go over each of these qualities, one at a time. Which of these qualities did the youth consistently rate as extremely important? Which did they consistently rate not important at all? Then focus on the very important qualities. How do friends who exhibit these qualities build one another up?

2. Invite volunteers to talk about friends who have helped them grow as a person or as a Christian. If you can, tell stories from your personal experience. Remind the youth that friends have a major influence on our attitudes, behaviors, and values, and that having supportive and trustworthy friends benefits us.

3. Answers may include the ability to forgive a friend (as in **Matthew 18:21-22**), willingness to make sacrifices on a friend's behalf (as in **John 15:13**), or patience and kindness (as in **1 Corinthians 13:4** and **Galatians 5:22**).

Look at the Book

Review the qualities of a good friend that you listed earlier in the warm-up activity and those lifted up while discussing the handout. Say: "Keep these qualities in mind while we look at a few Scriptures."

Ask volunteers to read aloud **Ruth 1:1-18** (the story of Ruth and Naomi), each person reading a few verses at a time. Tell the youth that according to **Deuteronomy 25:5-10,** widows were expected to marry their husbands' brothers. Since all of Naomi's sons are dead, Ruth and Naomi's other daughter-in-law, Orpah, have no brothers to marry and no reason to stay with their mother-in-law.

Then ask:

• How does this story show the qualities of a good friend we discussed earlier?

• Which of your friends is most like Ruth, willing to make sacrifices for your benefit?

• How, do you think, does Naomi feels when her daughter-in-law gives up the only life she has ever known to stay by her mother-in-law's side?

Then ask volunteers to read aloud **1 Samuel 18:1-9; 20:12-42** (the story of David and Jonathan), each person reading a few verses at a time. (Use *The Message* if you have it.) This is a lengthy Scripture, so you may want to stop occasionally to review what you've read.

Ask:

• How does this story show the qualities of a good friend we discussed earlier?

• How is Jonathan in this Scripture similar to and different from Ruth in the previous Scripture?

• How, do you think, does David feel when his best friend disobeys his father and endangers himself to save David's life?

Say: "Both Ruth and Jonathan exemplify what Jesus would later tell his disciples: 'No one has greater love than this, to lay down one's life for one's friends' (**John 15:13**). True friendships involve, among other things, sacrifice. And while we should forge relationships with friends who are willing to make sacrifices for us, we should also be willing to make sacrifices for them."

Wrap-up

Tell the youth to pay special attention this week to the positive qualities their friends possess, and challenge them to say a prayer of thanks each day for their friends. Also remind the youth that friendships must be mutual. Having strong, supportive friendships isn't simply a matter of finding people who are loving, patient, and respectful. We must treat our friends with the same love, patience, trust, and respect that we expect from them.

Close in prayer, asking God for the strength to be good friends and allowing for a time of silence during which the youth can say a prayer of thanks for their friends.